Think! Draw! Write! Level One

Grades 1-3

by Jean Marzollo and Katherine Martin Widmer

Published by Fearon Teacher Aids
an imprint of

McGraw-Hill
Children's Publishing

Credits

Authors: Jean Marzollo, Katherine Martin Widmer
Cover Design: Bill Nagel
Inside Illustrations: Katherine Martin Widmer
Page Design: Gustavo Medina

McGraw-Hill
Children's Publishing

A Division of The **McGraw-Hill** Companies

Published by Fearon Teacher Aids
An imprint of McGraw-Hill Children's Publishing
Copyright © 1982 Jean Marzollo and Katherine Martin Widmer

Send all inquiries to:
McGraw-Hill Children's Publishing
3195 Wilson Drive NW
Grand Rapids, Michigan 49544

Think! Draw! Write!, Level 1—grades 1–3
ISBN: 0-822-46946-4

Contents

Directions for Teachers

The purpose of these exercises is to motivate children to think creatively, focus on ideas by drawing them, write about the ideas with enthusiasm, and read their writing aloud or silently. The basic idea behind all the exercises is that writing can be fun.

There are various ways to use the exercise sheets. You can give them to children to use on their own during free time. You can assign them to children for homework. Or you can assign them for extra credit. In all of these cases, since the children basically will be working on their own, it makes sense to let the children choose the sheets they most like to do. This way, they will have the most fun and work at their creative best.

You can also use the sheets as a regular part of your writing curriculum. At a certain time of the day all children can work on the same exercise sheets. When the sheets are done, the children can share them either by reading them aloud to each other or by posting them on the bulletin board for everyone to see. Because all the children will be working on the same exercises, they should be encouraged to develop their own ideas and not copy another student's.

In cases where the children are not able to write down their own stories, have them dictate their stories to someone else who will print the words under the picture. This person can be a teacher, an aide, or an older child. Upper grade children can serve as tutors or helpers for younger children. Perhaps you can work out an arrangement with an upper grade class to meet regularly with your children for this purpose. Upper grade students who are working below their grade level may experience a great boost in morale when they see how much they can help a child who has not yet learned to write. Tell the tutor to write down the stories as the child tells them and not to change the child's wording, except when an obvious error is made. Explain that too much correcting can discourage young children from expressing themselves. When necessary, have the children continue their stories on the back of the exercise sheet.

If you are unable to write the children's stories for them or unable to arrange for someone else to do this at school, use the exercise sheets for oral storytelling in class. Then have the children take the exercise sheets home and ask a parent to write the words down.

The exercise sheets are organized loosely by content areas to help you use them most effectively in connection with the units in your curriculum. However, feel free to use the sheets in whatever order works best for you.

Draw a picture of how you look today. Then write a story about yourself today.

Use the other side.

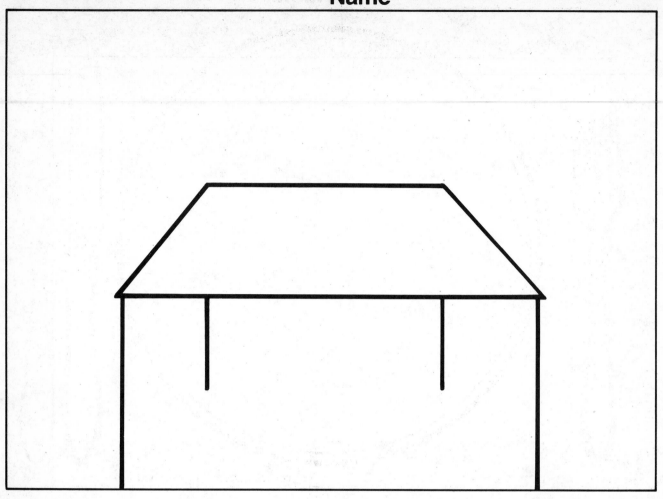

Draw a picture of your family eating dinner. Then write a story about your family at dinnertime.

Think! Draw! Write! 1   Copyright © 1982 by Marzollo and Widmer

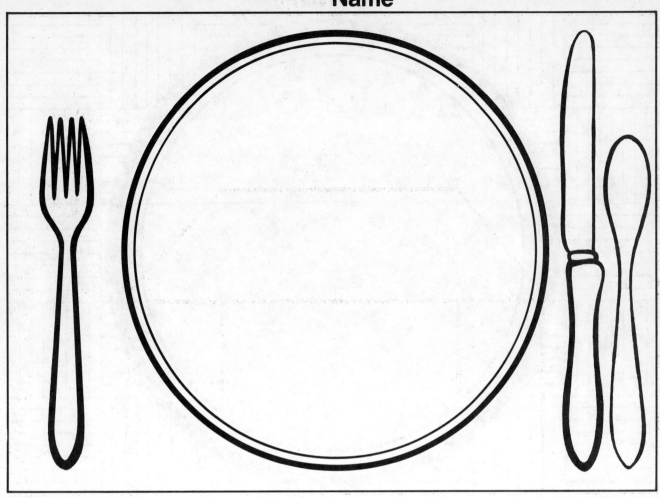

Draw the best meal you ever ate. Then write a story about it.

_____

— _____ —

— _____ —

— _____ —

— _____ —

— _____ —

— _____ —

— _____ —

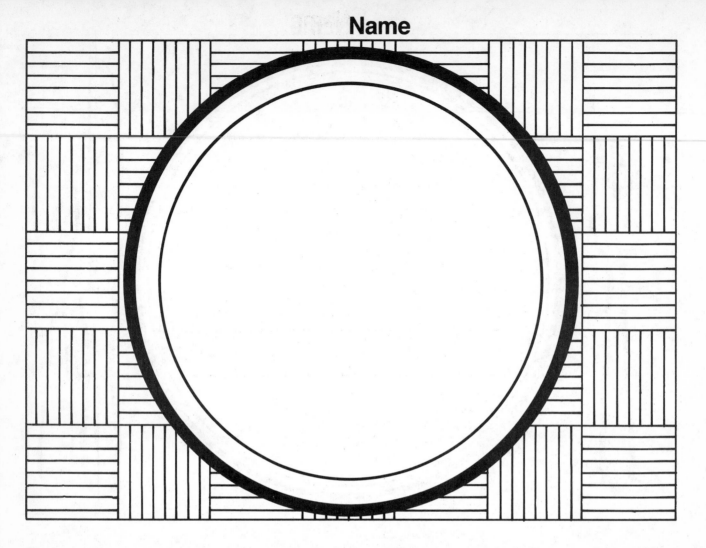

Draw the worst meal you ever ate. Then write a story about it.

_____

—   —
_____

—   —
_____

—   —
_____

—   —
_____

—   —
_____

—   —
_____

Think! Draw! Write! 1   Copyright © 1982 by Marzollo and Widmer

Use the other side.

Draw toys on these shelves in the toy store. Then write a story about buying them.

_____

—_____—

—_____—

_____

_____

_____

_____

_____

_____

_____

Use the other side.

Draw a dream you had when you were a baby. Then write a story about it.

_____

–   _____   –

_____

–   _____   –

_____

_____

–   _____   –

_____

_____

–   _____   –

_____

 Use the other side.

Think! Draw! Write! 1   Copyright © 1982 by Marzollo and Widmer

Draw what you think your mom or dad is doing right now.
Then write a story about it.

7

Use the other side.

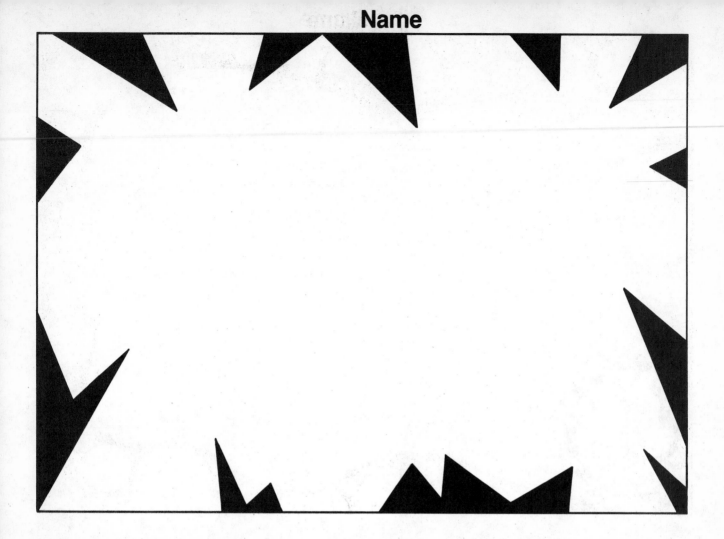

Draw the worst nightmare you ever had. Then write a story about it.

Think! Draw! Write! 1   Copyright © 1982 by Marzollo and Widmer

Use the other side.

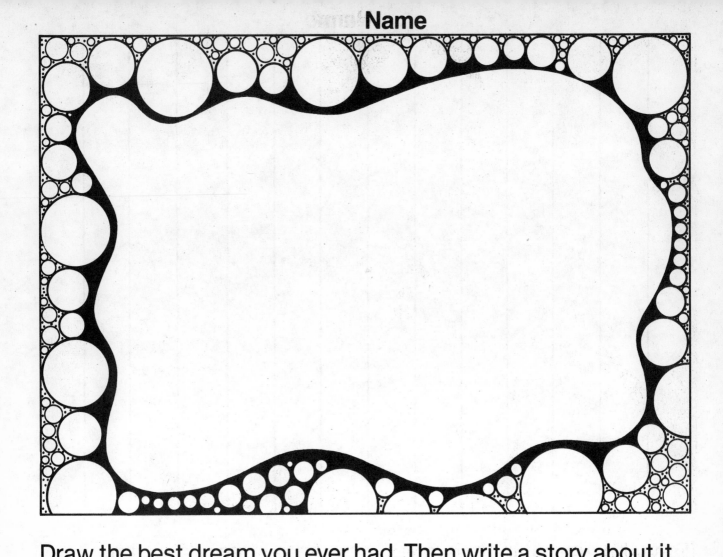

Draw the best dream you ever had. Then write a story about it.

Think! Draw! Write! 1   Copyright © 1982 by Marzollo and Widmer

_____

— _____ —

— _____ —

— _____ —

— _____ —

— _____ —

— _____ —

— _____ —

Use the other side.

Draw an animal in this cage. Then write a story about it.

Think! Draw! Write! 1   Copyright © 1982 by Marzollo and Widmer

Use the other side.

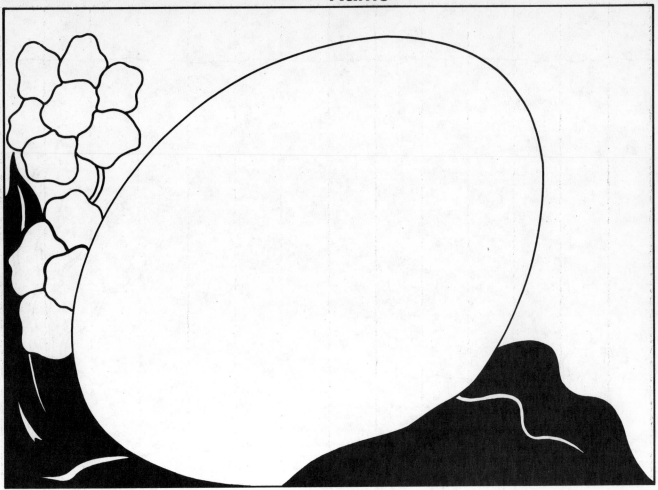

Draw a baby bird, turtle, snake, or dinosaur in this egg. Then write a story about it hatching.

_____

— _____ —

— _____ —

_____

— _____ —

_____

— _____ —

_____

— _____ —

_____

11   Use the other side.

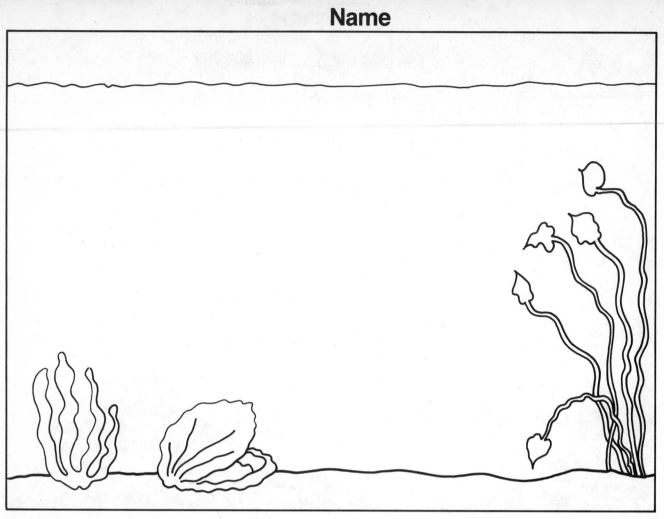

Draw fish in this fish tank. Then write a story about them.

_____

_____

_____

_____

_____

_____

_____

Think! Draw! Write! 1   Copyright © 1982 by Marzollo and Widmer

Use the other side.

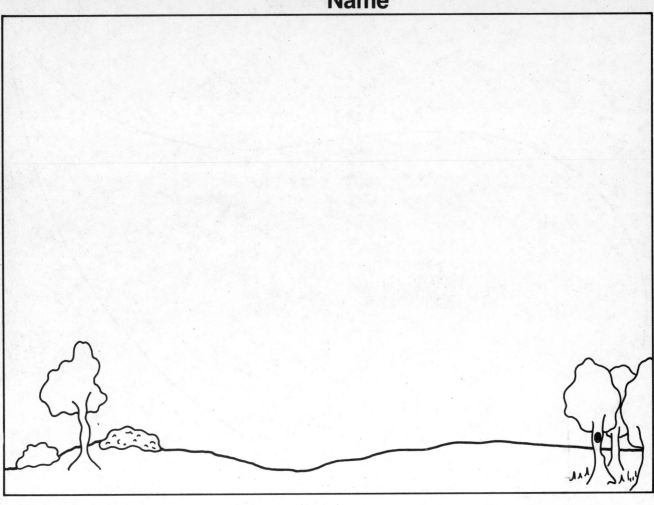

Draw a silly dinosaur called Sillysaurus. Then write a silly story about it.

_____

—_____—

—_____—

—_____—

—_____—

—_____—

—_____—

_____

Use the other side.

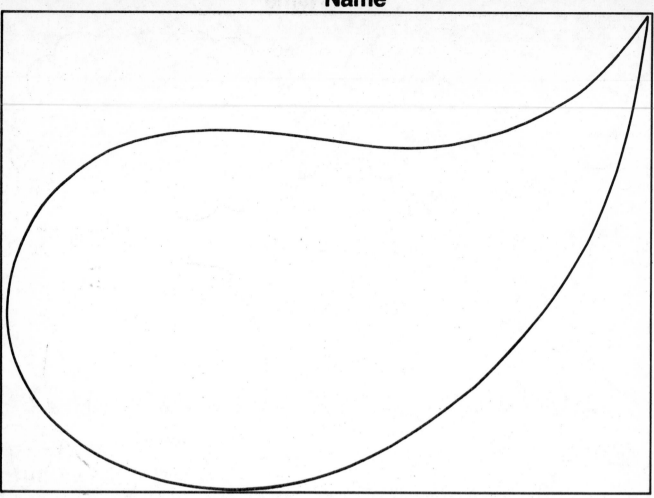

Draw yourself tiny enough to live inside a drop of water. Then write a story about your life there.

_____

—_____—

—_____—

—_____—

—_____—

—_____—

—_____—

—_____—

Think! Draw! Write! 1 Copyright © 1982 by Marzollo and Widmer

Draw a goldfish in the bowl. Draw a cat by the bowl. Write a story about what they might say to each other.

Use the other side.

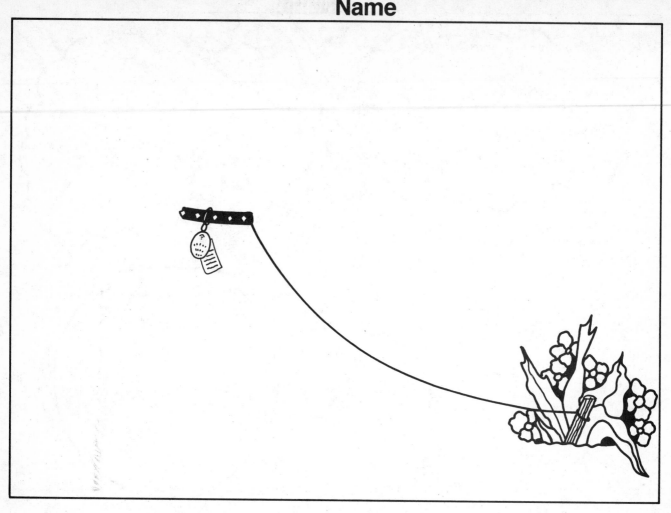

Draw a dog that fits in the collar. Write a story about the
collar breaking and the dog running away.

_____

— _____ —

_____

— _____ —

_____

— _____ —

_____

— _____ —

_____

— _____ —

_____

— _____ —

_____

Use the other side.

Think! Draw! Write! 1   Copyright © 1982 by Marzollo and Widmer

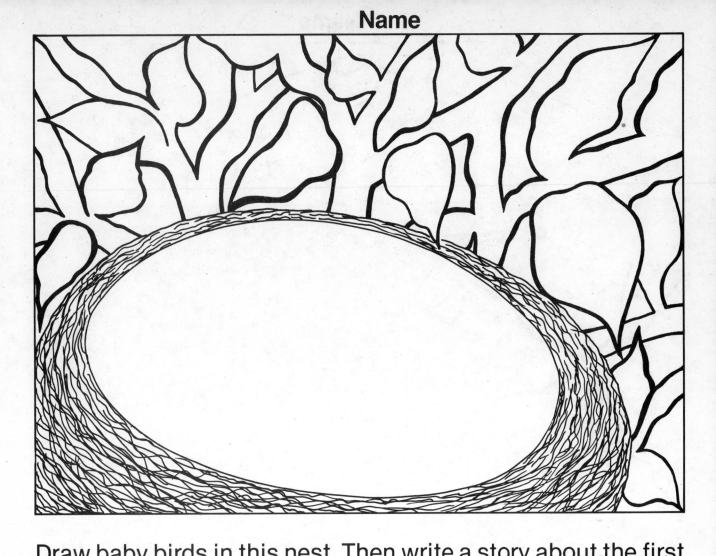

Draw baby birds in this nest. Then write a story about the first one of them that dares to fly.

Use the other side.

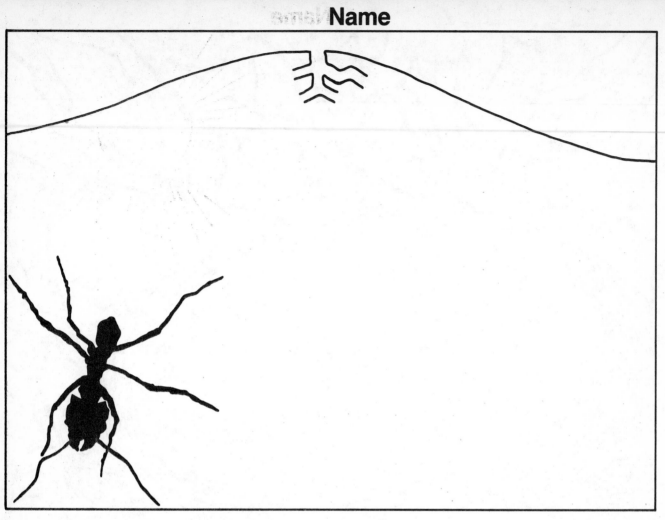

Draw the ants' underground tunnels. Then write a story about being an ant.

_____

_____

_____

_____

_____

_____

_____

_____

Use the other side.

Think! Draw! Write! 1   Copyright © 1982 by Marzollo and Widmer

Draw yourself on a sunny day. Then write a story about that day.

_____

— _____ —

— _____ —

— _____ —

— _____ —

— _____ —

— _____ —

_____

19   Use the other side.

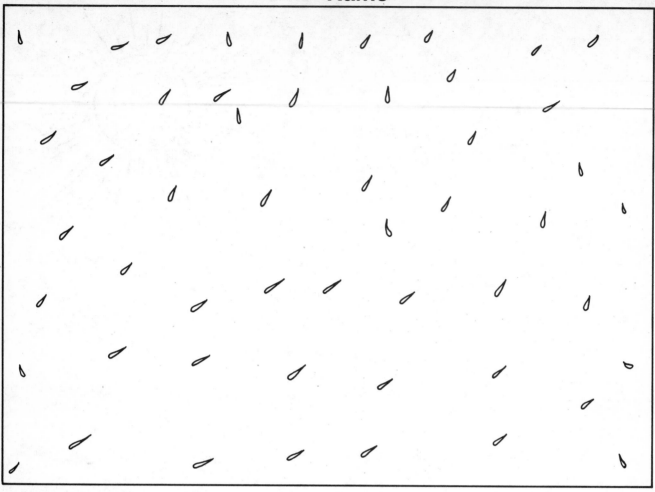

Draw yourself on a rainy day. Then write a story about that day.

Think! Draw! Write! 1   Copyright © 1982 by Marzollo and Widmer

Use the other side.

Draw yourself on a snowy day. Then write a story about that day.

Use the other side.

Draw a garden you would like to grow. Then write a story about it.

Think! Draw! Write! 1   Copyright © 1982 by Marzollo and Widmer

Use the other side.

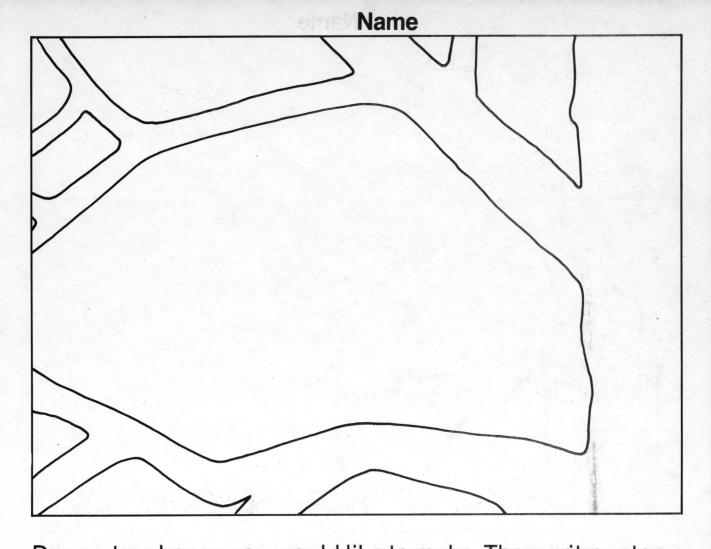

Draw a tree house you would like to make. Then write a story about it.

_____

—_____—

—_____—

—_____—

—_____—

—_____—

—_____—

_____

Use the other side.

Draw a good place for people to put their garbage. Then write
a story about it.

Think! Draw! Write! 1   Copyright © 1982 by Marzollo and Widmer

Use the other side.

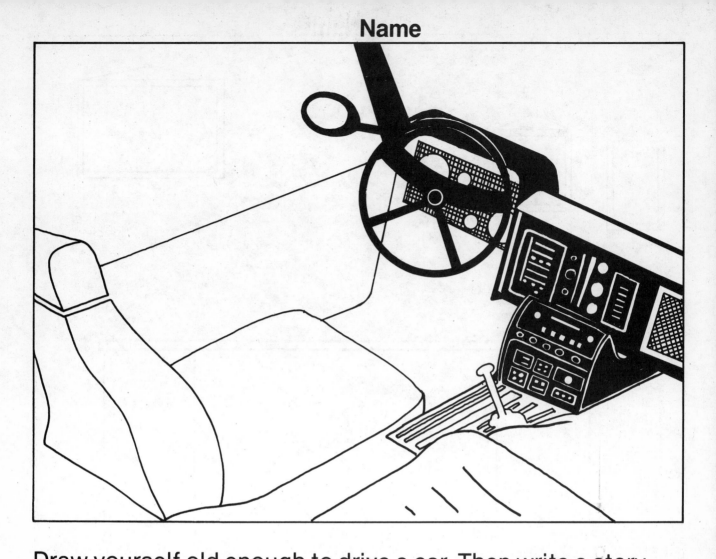

Draw yourself old enough to drive a car. Then write a story about driving.

Use the other side.

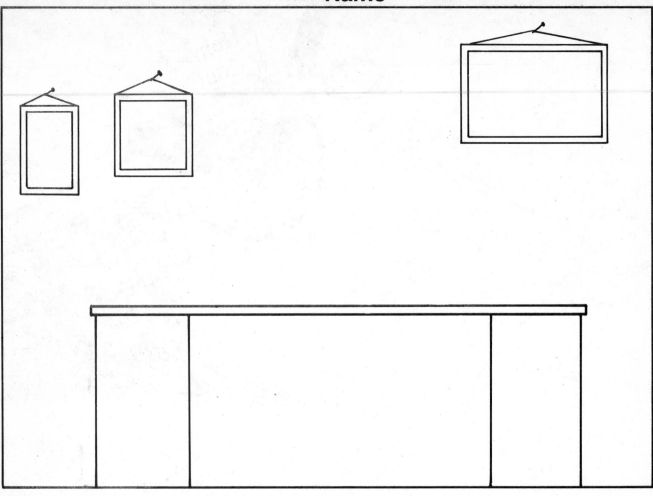

Draw yourself old enough to work in an office. This is your
desk. Then write a story about your job.

Think! Draw! Write! 1 Copyright © 1982 by Marzollo and Widner

Use the other side.

Draw something real that scares you. Then write a story about it.

_____

- _____ -

- _____ -

- _____ -

_____

- _____ -

- _____ -

Use the other side.

Draw something *not* real that scares you anyway. Then write a story about it.

_____
—   —
_____
—   —
_____
—   —
_____
—   —
_____
—   —
_____
—   —
_____

Use the other side.

Think! Draw! Write! 1   Copyright © 1982 by Marzollo and Widmer

Draw yourself landing on Mars. Then write a story about what happened.

Think! Draw! Write! 1   Copyright © 1982 by Marzollo and Widmer

 Use the other side.

Draw yourself in these magic sneakers. Then write a story about where you will go in them.

_____

—   _____   —

—   _____   —

—   _____   —

_____

—   _____   —

—   _____   —

Think! Draw! Write! 1   Copyright © 1982 by Marzollo and Widmer

Use the other side.

Draw a big magic wand in this wizard's hand. Then write a story about the wizard and the wand.

Use the other side.

This is the front door of your magic castle. Draw the rest of the castle. Then write a story about it.

_____

— _____ —

— _____ —

— _____ —

— _____ —

— _____ —

— _____ —

Think! Draw! Write! 1   Copyright © 1982 by Marzollo and Widmer

Use the other side.

Pretend you can fly above the clouds. Draw what you see.
Then write a story about it.

_____

— _____ —

_____

— _____ —

_____

— _____ —

_____

— _____ —

_____

— _____ —

_____

— _____ —

Use the other side.

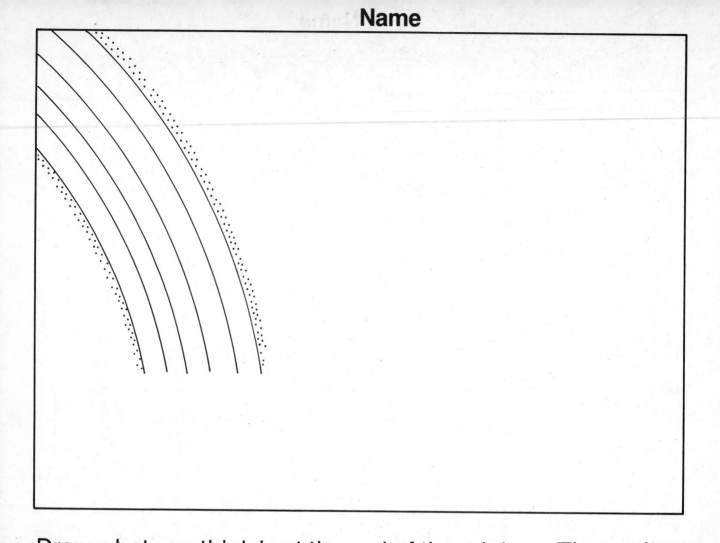

Draw what you think is at the end of the rainbow. Then write a story about finding it.

Think! Draw! Write! 1   Copyright © 1982 by Marzollo and Widmer

Use the other side.

Make this into a haunted house. Then write a story about it.

Use the other side.

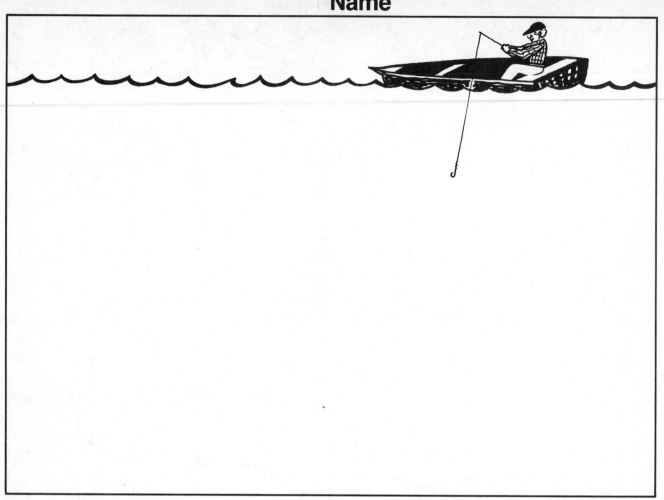

Draw a monster swimming under the boat. Then write a story about catching it.

_____
_____
_____
_____
_____
_____
_____
_____
_____
_____

Use the other side.

Think! Draw! Write! 1 Copyright © 1982 by Marzollo and Widmer

Dress yourself in a Halloween costume. Then write a story about yourself on Halloween night.

_____

— _____ —

_____

— _____ —

_____

— _____ —

_____

— _____ —

_____

Use the other side.

Draw two things you are thankful for. Then write a story about both of them.

Think! Draw! Write! 1   Copyright © 1982 by Marzollo and Widmer

Use the other side.

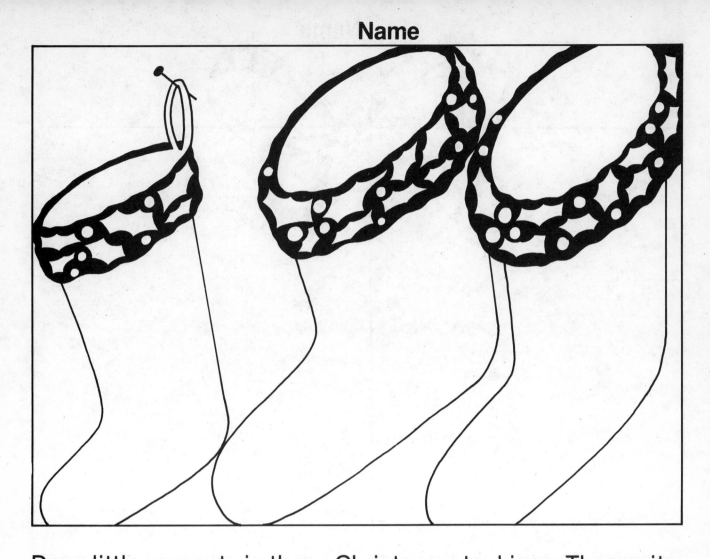

Draw little presents in these Christmas stockings. Then write a story about how they got there.

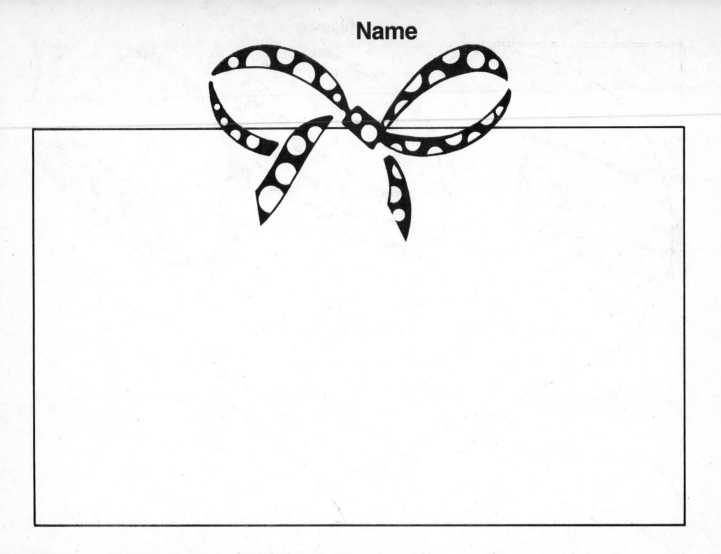

Draw what's inside this box. Then write a story about who will get the present.

_____
_____
_____
_____
_____
_____
_____
_____

Use the other side.

Think! Draw! Write! 1.   Copyright © 1982 by Marzollo and Widmer

Draw a valentine for someone you love. Then write a story about giving it.

_____

—   _____   —

—   _____   —

—   _____   —

—   _____   —

—   _____   —

—   _____   —

—   _____

Use the other side.

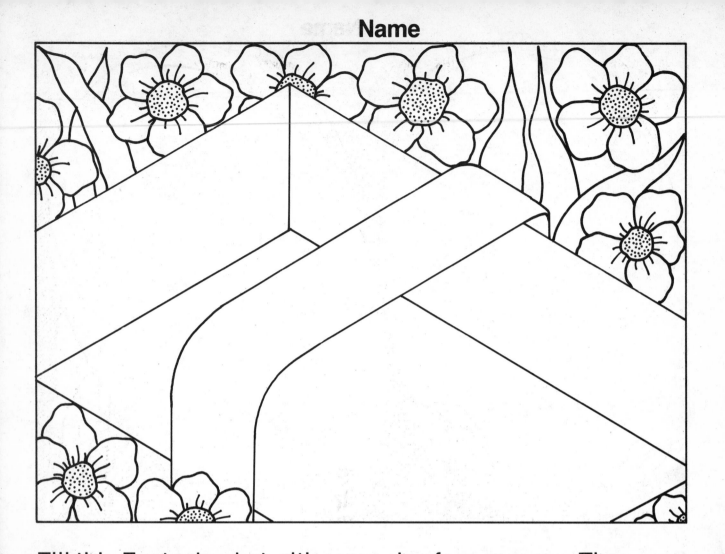

Fill this Easter basket with a surprise for someone. Then write a story about giving it.

_____

‐ _____ ‐

‐ _____ ‐

‐ _____ ‐

‐ _____ ‐

‐ _____ ‐

‐ _____ ‐

‐ _____ ‐

_____

Think! Draw! Write! 1   Copyright © 1982 by Marzollo and Widmer

Use the other side.

Decorate these two eggs for someone you love. Then write a story about hiding them.

_____

_____

_____

_____

_____

_____

_____

_____

_____

_____

Use the other side.

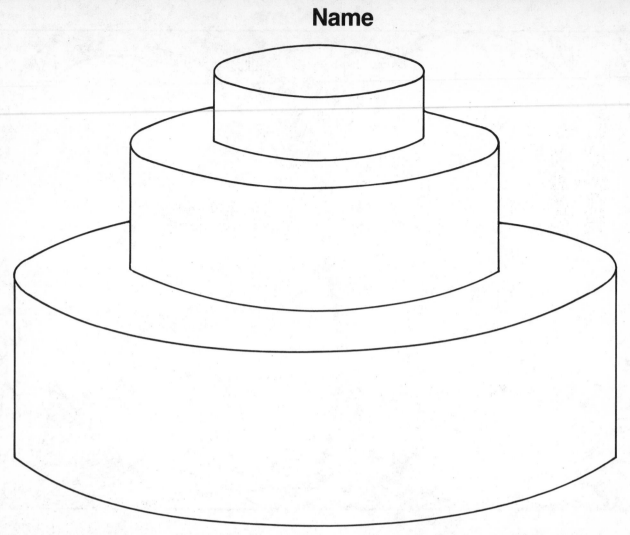

Decorate this birthday cake for yourself. Then write a story about your birthday.

_____

- _____ -

_____

- _____ -

_____

- _____ -

_____

- _____ -

_____

- _____ -

_____

Use the other side.